Original title:
The Great Purpose Search: Take 2

Copyright © 2025 Creative Arts Management OÜ
All rights reserved.

Author: Christian Leclair
ISBN HARDBACK: 978-1-80566-284-6
ISBN PAPERBACK: 978-1-80566-579-3

The Great Awakening

In a world so bright and cheery,
We search for answers, feeling eerie.
With coffee cups stacked to the sky,
We ponder if pie is the reason why.

Woke up today with socks unmatched,
Are these signs our future's hatched?
Chasing dreams that make us laugh,
Like cats who chase the sunlight's path.

Patterns of Existence

Life's a quilt of crazy threads,
Stitched with hope and silly spreads.
We find meaning in pizza slices,
And argue if toppings are the wisest.

Kites fly high in a reckless dance,
Like kids with no sense of circumstance.
Patterns form in a spaghetti mess,
As we ponder life with some finesse.

The Pulse of Creation

Bouncing balls of cosmic fluff,
Scribbling notes that say, "Don't huff!"
In the lab where dreams collide,
Spaghetti monsters take a wild ride.

Tickle your brain, feel the pulse,
As we wriggle and giggle with convulse.
With crayons in hand and chaos in mind,
We draw the fun that we hope to find.

A Traveler's Reflection

On a journey with shoes untied,
I trip over wisdom, like I've tried.
Road signs wink, and GPS smirks,
As I chase down the meaning that lurks.

With my backpack full of snacky dreams,
Life is sweeter than it seems.
I meet my thoughts like old friends,
Laughing 'til the journey ends.

The Map of Echoes

In a land where echoes giggle,
A map was drawn, not quite a wiggle.
X marks the spot where laughs collide,
With treasure chests that joke and slide.

The compass spins with glee and cheer,
Finding paths that lead to beer.
Each twist and turn, a ticklish fate,
As clowns join in—oh, what a state!

A riddle here, a pun there,
Navigating through the silly air.
Where rubber chickens lead the way,
And whoopee cushions always stay.

So grab your friends, let's roam about,
In this land where no one pouts.
With laughter echoing through the trees,
We'll map our tomfoolery with ease.

Unraveling Destiny

In a world where socks play hide-and-seek,
Destiny's just a game for the cheek.
With each untangled knot, we find,
A purpose wrapped in fun, so blind.

Throw your plans to the dogs, they bark,
Chasing tails, they leave a mark.
As life unfolds in jests and jives,
Who knew that chaos helps us thrive?

With silly hats upon our heads,
We stumble forward, no sense of dread.
Each misstep, a comic show,
Where laughter leads, we gladly go.

So let us twirl in this grand design,
Where every laugh is truly divine.
Together we'll create our fate,
In the dance of life, no time to wait.

Reflections on Meaning

Why does the toaster eat bread?
Only it knows what's in its head.
I'm on a quest, in socks and shoes,
To find my place and dodge the blues.

Maps are useless, I just get lost,
Like a dog who forgot what it tossed.
Chasing meaning like a cat chases yarn,
Missing the point, but finding some charm.

Navigating the Waters of Life

I've set sail on a paper boat,
With a peanut for a sailor's coat.
Waves of thoughts that splash and sway,
Distraction's the captain leading astray.

Navigational skills? Far from prime,
I once got lost, oh, never a crime!
I'll fish for truth with a noodle string,
Catch the essence, or maybe a fling.

The Canvas of Ambitions

My canvas sprawls with paint and dreams,
Yet I drop my brush, or so it seems.
Messy splatters, colors gone wild,
Like a toddler trying art, oh so mild.

Brush strokes whisper, "What's your goal?"
While my thoughts jostle, out of control.
A masterpiece or just a joke?
In pursuit of meaning, a laugh I stoke.

Searching for the Light

With a flashlight shining in the day,
I search for wisdom, come what may.
Rabbits hop, wearing shades and hats,
While I trip over invisible mats.

A beacon calls, but where's the glow?
Maybe it's hiding, just like my dough.
Chasing shadows, I run with delight,
In the laughter of seeking, I find my light.

Embracing the Unknown

I wandered in a field of dreams,
Where cows gave sage advice, it seems.
I asked them, 'What's the meaning here?'
They said, 'Just moo and persevere!'

With every step, I tripped and fell,
On things I thought were wise to tell.
Like who put socks inside the sink?
And why the bathroom smells like ink?

Fragments of a Higher Truth

I pondered deep, lost in my head,
While ice cream melted on my bed.
Mysteries wrapped in waffle cones,
And deep insights hidden in phone ringtones.

The universe speaks in riddles and quirks,
Like why do cats prefer to lurk?
I scribbled thoughts, but it was late,
My pen turned into a slice of fate.

Threads of Connection

I called my friend and lost my way,
Asked for help on this fine day.
He laughed and said, 'You're on your phone!'
'But where's the pizza?' I sighed alone.

Connections found in pizza crumbs,
In laughter shared, and silly hums.
We're all just threads in a wacky quilt,
Made of dreams and soda spilt.

Navigating Life's Labyrinth

In this maze where I lose my mind,
I search for snacks of all kinds.
A sign reads 'Laugh,' but I take a wrong turn,
And stumble on lessons I never learned.

A minotaur in slippers, oh what a sight,
He offered me chips and said, 'Take a bite.'
Life's twists may twist and turn amiss,
But chocolate hides in the labyrinth bliss.

The Compass Within

Lost amidst my laundry pile,
I found my compass, oh what a style!
Pointing to the fridge, never to roam,
In search of snacks, it leads me home.

Maps all tangled in a mix,
Guided by a craving fix.
Where's the path to nacho cheese?
My compass wobbles; it aims to please.

Friends say, "Dude, find your way!"
But I just want to eat today.
With ice cream as my guiding star,
Who needs directions? I'll go far!

Round and round, I chase a treat,
With every twist, I taste defeat.
Yet laughter leads my merry quest,
For in fun, I am truly blessed.

Notes from the Soul's Voyage

In search of wisdom, I packed my bag,
With a spoon and fork, oh what a drag!
Wrote a note on a napkin too,
"Avoid deep thoughts, they make you stew!"

The map got lost, the boat still floats,
With crumbs of donuts and half-eaten oats.
I scribble questions on a plate,
"Where's the cake? Is it too late?"

Sailing on the sea of despair,
I see a rubber duck, floating with flair.
It quacks, it floats, it shares the day,
Life's true treasures come out to play.

So here's my note to the wandering soul,
Pack snacks and laughter, that's the goal!
For in the mess of our grand ride,
Joyful chaos is what's inside.

In Pursuit of the Infinite

Chasing dreams through fields of cheese,
Racing thoughts float like a breeze.
If infinite means vast and wide,
Do I get there on a pogo ride?

My to-do list is far too grand,
With fidget spinners in my hand.
One hop forward, two steps back,
Infinite snack breaks? That's on track!

Invisible goals in my rearview,
Dodging wisdom like a kangaroo.
Life's a puzzle, or so they say,
But I'm just here to play all day.

With each laugh, I lose my way,
But isn't that the game we play?
To chase the infinite, be blissfully free,
With twinkling eyes and a slice of brie!

Reflections on a Winding Path

With paths so twisted, I stroll and sway,
Wearing mismatched socks, hip hip hooray!
Each step leads to a brand-new song,
Do I dance, or do I schlong?

Mirrors reflect my puzzled expression,
I ponder snacktime as my obsession.
Should I turn left or just go straight?
Finding snacks, that's my fate!

Friends join in with a wink and shout,
"What's this route? Give us a route!"
We laugh and skip as squirrels dance by,
Chasing crumbs as we flutter nigh.

In the end, it's just a game,
As long as laughter stays the same.
On a winding path, we'll twirl and spin,
Finding joy in the chaos within.

Chasing Fleeting Shadows

In a world where shadows grinned,
I chased them down, I thought I'd win.
But they just laughed and did a twirl,
While I tripped over my own swirl.

With feet like clowns and arms akimbo,
I stumbled past the old bamboo.
A puppet show of my own design,
With every shadow, I'd intertwine.

Awakening the Inner Compass

I set my sights on north and south,
My compass broke, I lost my mouth!
With maps of pizza and tales of pie,
I flagged down ducks as they waddled by.

'Yo, Mr. Duck, which way to fun?'
He quacked a laugh and said, 'Just run!'
So off I went, a sprinting fool,
Guided by quacks, I'm nobody's tool.

The Map of Dreams

I drew a map of dreams with flair,
But smeared some ketchup; now it's rare.
The treasure's in the fridge, so bold,
With moldy cheese and crusty old gold.

An X marked a spot of spilled hot tea,
With chickens dancing, wild and free.
Every 'X' leads to breakfast treats,
In a quest where pancakes sound like beats.

Beyond the Veil of Ordinary

Behind the door marked 'Nowhere here,'
I found a cake with a face and cheer.
It told me tales of socks on shoes,
In a land where jellybeans are blues.

A dragon served coffee, hot and sweet,
While squirrels in bow ties danced to the beat.
With farts as symphonies echoing near,
Extraordinary lived, oh so queer!

Flames of Aspiration

In a world without a map,
We chase our dreams in a snap.
With socks that don't quite match,
And plans that always scratch.

We leap like flying fish,
Upon a cosmic dish.
With coffee in our hands,
And tinfoil on our bands.

From banana peels we slip,
Yet never lose our grip.
With laughter as our guide,
We surf on joy, not pride.

On roller skates we glide,
Through worlds that twist and slide.
While ducks quack in delight,
We're off into the night.

Beneath the Surface of Dreams

Beneath the waves of thought,
Funny fish we've caught.
In tangled nets we find,
Witty wisdom intertwined.

With anchors made of cheese,
We sail with greatest ease.
While jellyfish play cards,
We dance among the yards.

A searchlight made of fries,
Illuminates our skies.
With giggles on the breeze,
We sail the seas with ease.

The Odyssey of Intent

To the left of 'maybe' land,
There's a ship with a rubber band.
Sailing softly on a whim,
With a crew that's full of him.

While the squirrels take the helm,
We navigate the realm.
With maps drawn in crayon bright,
We journey into the night.

With treasure chests of puns,
And laughter at the runs,
With fish that sings our songs,
The adventure never wrongs.

Fables of the Forgotten

Beneath the tales of lore,
Are giggles at the core.
With frogs that wear bow ties,
And hats that sing their lies.

We tell of quests gone wild,
Where wisdom is a child.
A parrot with a speech,
Recites the things we teach.

In riddles of the past,
Where joys are built to last.
We dance through time's embrace,
With laughter on our face.

Heartbeats of the Universe

In a cosmic dance, stars trip and fall,
Earth winks back, as if to call.
Galaxies giggle, spinning with glee,
While black holes burp in celestial spree.

Asteroids juggle, comets take flight,
Planets play tag, from day into night.
Even the sun cracks a cheeky grin,
Warming our hearts, inviting us in.

A quasar sneezes, whoops—there goes time!
"Catch me if you can!" it shouts, oh so prime.
Cosmic clowns, with tricks up their sleeves,
Leave us in stitches, as we just believe.

So next time you ponder, don't take it all slow,
The universe laughs, let your joy overflow!
With heartbeats that tick in a comical way,
The cosmos is jesting, come laugh and play!

Lingering Questions

Why did the chicken cross the void?
To find out if it's truly enjoyed!
Do aliens eat baked beans on toast?
Or are they just waiting for Earth to boast?

Is life just a game of cosmic charades?
Where every answered question just evades?
If we asked the stars for a sign or two,
Would they wink back, or avoid the view?

What's the meaning of socks that disappear?
Do they dance in the dryer, or drink too much beer?
Are we but marionettes in a grand puppet show?
While popcorn awaits for the main act to grow?

Oh, ponder, my friend, these riddles so bright,
As laughter is born in the depths of the night.
Join in the jest, embrace silly fears,
For in questioning life, we find the good cheers!

Labors of the Spirit

A ghost in a café sips sassy lattes,
While pondering life like it's all simply fates.
With waffles of wisdom stacked high on a plate,
It moans, "Can spirits even gain weight?"

Meditating in slippers, what a sight to behold,
Floating on clouds with intentions so bold.
Minds on a treadmill, running nowhere fast,
"Can we skip to the end?" the spirits all gasp.

They've got errands to run, like shopping for peace,
But the sale on good vibes? They just can't cease.
It's a labor of giggles, a hustle of fun,
Finding laughter, oh yes, it's never quite done!

So let's all join these spirits, in joy they abound,
For life's the best labor, when laughter is found.
With sprightly steps, dance through the air,
In the spirit's sweet play, we're all aware!

Fractals of Purpose

In the garden of meaning, plants twist and twirl,
Each leaf holds a secret, like a pearl.
"Is that a dandelion dreaming to be,
A lion or a puppy?" asks a bee.

Fractals of purpose, in patterns so bright,
Spirals of laughter flutter into the night.
Each question a petal, unfolding the truth,
With silly designs, like a kid's tooth.

A cactus debates with a wandering vine,
"Do we exist for the sun, or just for the wine?"
With roots intertwined, arguing their case,
While a potato chuckles, "I'm comfortable, face!"

So dance through these fractals, explore every bend,
Life's a puzzle where laughter won't end.
In the cosmic garden, just let curiosity lead,
With purpose in giggles, come plant every seed!

Echoes of the Past

In a room full of socks, I thought I would find,
A treasure, a gem, or a purpose aligned.
But alas, just a mismatch, the odd and the free,
Who knew life's big answers were stuck by a tee?

Grandma's old stories, a laugh and a sigh,
Like a cat chasing shadows, oh where did they fly?
Wisdom in jest, yet serious too,
Finding my fortune in a tip of my shoe.

A clock with no hands, just ticking away,
Tells me with giggles, "Go out and play!"
If I can't find my purpose, just throw me a snack,
The cake of existence is never too slack.

So here's to the clues that we follow with cheer,
In distractions we wander, and feel them quite near.
The past holds a chuckle, a wink in the night,
We dance with our ghosts until morning's first light.

The Uncharted Soul

An inner explorer, just sipping my tea,
Mapping the depths of my own quirky spree.
With a compass that wiggles, and a map made of cheese,
I laugh through the chaos, a map made to please.

Through jungles of laundry and mountains of socks,
Navigate nonsense, ignoring the clocks.
A treasure hunt beckons, with pie at the end,
Finding myself while I follow my friend.

The uncharted waters of my morning toast,
I toast to the burns, they matter the most.
Each bite a new journey, absurd yet divine,
Exploring the kitchen, where all is just fine.

Dive deep in the ice cream, swim in the sprinkles,
Laughing with joy as each flavor tinkles.
Map out the giggles, and dance with no goal,
In the silly adventures, I find my own soul.

Tides of Transformation

The waves greet my toes, with a splish and a splash,
As I ponder my purpose, all wild in a flash.
With crabs in my pocket, and seaweed for hair,
I transform like a jellyfish, floating without care.

A sandcastle built with dreams made of cream,
Collapses quite easily, or so it would seem.
But I laugh at the wreckage, a giggle or two,
Tides crash and recede, but I'm still in the queue.

Seagulls are squawking their plans for the day,
While I'm here just wondering if I should play.
With the moon as my buddy, we'll dance on the shore,
Finding joy in the muck, who could ask for more?

So here's to the oceans, the tides that will shift,
I may not find wisdom, but at least I can drift.
In waves of confusion, the laughter will churn,
For in this wild ocean, my spirit will learn.

Labyrinthine Journeys

A maze made of mirrors, reflecting my face,
I wander in circles, a comical race.
Should I follow the left? Or perhaps to the right?
The echoes of laughter keep me up at night.

A Minotaur snores between IKEA and dream,
As I grab on to breadcrumbs like the world's greatest scheme.
I trip on my shoelaces, a tumble and roll,
Yet joy in the goofiness deepens my soul.

With every wrong turn, I pick up a joke,
New punchlines are waiting; it's all in the poke.
Finding my way through the twists and the bends,
Each folly a lesson, with giggles as friends.

So if you should wander this maze of delight,
Just follow the laughter, it'll guide you right.
Through the twists and the turns, embody the fun,
In the labyrinth's heart, you'll discover the sun.

Embracing the Undefined

In a world where socks go missing,
I ponder life while slightly hissing.
Why do spoons have a way to hide?
Maybe purpose is where we decide.

Chasing coffee in a paper cup,
Finding answers while I trip up.
Did I lock the door? Oh, wait and see,
This could be the key! Or just my knee.

The Quest Unraveled

One day I thought, let's seek the truth,
But tripped on my cat—such a sleuth!
With every step, a new riddle's tossed,
Am I the seeker, or just lost?

Maps are scribbles, my thoughts a stew,
I'll ask a squirrel, he seems insightful too.
Is my destiny tied to this game,
Or just my fridge, calling my name?

Chasing the Divine Spark

I chased a spark with a pint in hand,
Was it wisdom or just a grain of sand?
With laughter as my guiding light,
I danced around, a silly sight.

My shoes untied, with popcorn in tow,
Who knew that laughter helps us grow?
The more I search, the more I find,
The best of times are hilariously blind.

Reverberations of the Heart

My heart beats like a drummer late,
In the quest for pizza, I contemplate.
Do I follow dreams or just the dough?
Life's a comedy, with each new show.

Each giggle echoes, a symphony wild,
In the madness, I am a child.
With joy as my compass, I will embark,
To find the spark in every quirk.

Footprints in the Sand

I walked along the beach one day,
With not a clue, just passing play.
A seagull squawked, my hat flew high,
I chased it down, oh me, oh my!

The tide rolled in, my footprints gone,
A crab waved back, its dance was fun.
I wondered then, did I make my mark?
Or did it wash away, just like a spark?

A dolphin leapt, as if to say,
"Life's a game, come join the fray!"
I laughed and dove, a splashy act,
While all my worries faded, cracked.

So next time life feels like a blur,
Just add some fun, let laughter stir.
With every wave, embrace the spree,
And leave behind your worries—free!

Revelations at Dawn

At dawn, I found my coffee cold,
My dreams were made of tales retold.
A squirrel chatted, with such delight,
"Have you seen my stash? It's out of sight!"

The sun peeked in, a golden goof,
While shadows danced upon the roof.
I struck a pose, for what it's worth,
"Is this a sign? Am I of worth?"

A crow cawed loud, as if to jest,
"Your purpose found? You take a rest!"
I tipped my hat, and laughed aloud,
Surrounded by life, I felt so proud.

With birds in chorus, I made my way,
Revelations came, in their own play.
Each silly thought, a clue I trace,
In every chuckle, I find my place!

Flickers of Hope

In the dark, a light blinked bright,
I waved my hands, what a silly sight!
Is it a firefly, or a distant star?
I'll chase it down, wherever you are!

A cat nearby, its eyes aglow,
"Don't chase the glow, just let it flow!"
But who can resist a twinkling tease?
I stumbled over branches, playing with ease.

With every flicker, a twist of fate,
Could it be luck, or something great?
I danced like a fool, with joy in the air,
Finding joy in glitches, without a care.

So if you spot a spark tonight,
Join in the fun, take flight, feel light.
For purpose hides in laughter's leap,
And in those moments, your heart shall keep!

The Dance of Purpose

A party started under the moon,
Where purpose gathered, a merry tune.
I tripped on my feet, in rhythm untrue,
But every fall, brought laughter anew.

With friends all around, we spun and kicked,
Creating chaos, our feet all mixed.
A dog joined in, with a wagging tail,
As if to say, "Let's never bail!"

The stars applauded, with their bright glow,
Joining our dance, putting on a show.
Through every misstep, we found our groove,
Purpose is laughter, it's how we move.

So sway with joy, let your heart dance free,
In the oddest moments, it's bliss you'll see.
With each silly twirl, you'll find your way,
In the hilarious dance, live for today!

Journey Beyond the Horizon

Woke up today with glee,
Off to find what's meant for me.
A sandwich in my pocket tight,
But where's the map? It gives me fright.

The sun is shining, birds do sing,
I skip along, it's a funny thing.
Fell in a puddle, oh what a sight,
But I'll just laugh, it feels so right.

Clouds above begin to play,
Dancing shapes that lead my way.
A cow in sunglasses by the road,
Is this the path? I hit 'record'.

I met a turtle, slow but wise,
Said, "Take your time, enjoy the skies."
I waved goodbye on that crazy ride,
Turns out my purpose is silly pride!

Whispers of the Heart's Desire

I sat and pondered by the creek,
What does my heart truly seek?
A donut shop, a chocolate treat,
Or some place where I can beat my feet?

Banana peels, they made me slip,
Down the path, I did a flip.
Laughter echoed through the trees,
I think my heart just wants some cheese.

A squirrel approached with a grand plan,
To write a book entitled "Be a Fan!"
But I just chuckled, said, "Not today,"
I'm on a quest for fun and play.

So off I went, with snacks in hand,\nSearching for laughter, oh, isn't it grand?
With every step, more giggles arise,
Life's purpose tucked in joy and pies!

The Unseen Map

I woke one morn with a grand design,
To find my way, or at least some wine.
An old, crumpled map in my hand,
Turns out it leads to a dessert stand.

With arrows pointing left and right,
I headed out, no end in sight.
A dog chased me down, barking loud,
Is he my guide or just too proud?

I asked a raccoon for advice,
He stole my snack - now that's not nice!
But he did wink and jiggle around,
Maybe the purpose is to jump and bound?

So I danced along, the world turned bright,
With twists and turns, it felt just right.
I found joy hidden where I least think,
Along this road, my heart can't shrink!

Revelations in the Silence

In quiet moments, giggles creep,
Life's funny secrets start to leap.
I sat real still, a bug on my nose,
To find my purpose, I struck a pose!

The wind started whispering tales unshared,
Of sock gnomes and clowns, no one dared.
My chair squeaked loud, the silence broke,
Maybe I'm meant for a silly joke?

Clouds drifted by, making faces galore,
Laughing so hard, I fell on the floor.
A hidden truth in giggles bright,
That maybe life's purpose is pure delight.

So I'll embrace the quiet sound,
In all the laughter, true joy is found.
With open arms, I'll take a chance,
To skip and twirl in a silly dance!

Sculpting the Future

With clay in hand, I shape my fate,
A lumpy mug that just won't wait.
I thought I'd make a sleek new plate,
But ended up with 'Oops!' on my slate.

The wheel spins fast, it's quite a dance,
My masterpiece? A lopsided glance.
A sculpture that provokes a chance,
To giggle at my creative romance.

Each crack and crevice tells a tale,
Of how I tripped and almost fell.
With laughter echoing, I unveil,
A wobbly pot, but oh so swell!

So here I sit, my hands in clay,
Attempting art in a silly way.
Who knew that life would go this way,
With laughs and gaffes at every sway?

The Echo of Choices

I stood at the fork, a wild spree,
One side promised sweets, the other, a tree.
I chose the cake, sweet destiny,
But ended up stuck—a bee buzzed at me!

The choices I make, a comical spree,
Like picking a movie with buddies so free.
"Not that one!" they shout, "It's as dull as a bee!"
We settle for films where turtles agree.

In life's little maze, I wander and roam,
Each step leads me, not far from home.
But each turn I take, I've got my own gnome,
Who giggles and trips, but calls it sweet chrome!

So I chuckle and grin, as choices clash,
With every wrong turn, creating a splash.
I've learned one thing, through all this brash,
Life's a jest, and I'm here for the bash!

Seeking the Hidden Treasure

With a map that's drawn in crayon blue,
I set off to find a treasure or two.
Through muddy patches and the gooey dew,
I tripped on a rock and said, "Who knew?"

X marked the spot—a dog's resting place,
I chased off the cat, with a laugh on my face.
Then found three bones—what a hilarious chase!
The treasure I seek is a curious case!

A chest full of socks? Or candy galore?
In my quest for gold, I've found much more.
Laughter and joy, what my heart will score,
With friends all around, we'll always explore!

So pass me the map, let's start this charade,
In search of lost fortunes that will surely fade.
For the real hidden treasure? It's in the parade,
Of memories we make, and the fun that we've laid!

Beneath Life's Surface

Beneath the waves, I seek a pearl,
But all I find is a seaweed swirl.
A fish in a hat does a little twirl,
While I search for treasures in the ocean's whirl.

With goggles on tight and flippers too wide,
I fumble and splash, trying to glide.
The fish chuckle softly, it's hard to hide,
Their laughter surrounds me; oh, what a ride!

I sift through sand, uncover a shoe,
It belonged to a crab who wished he flew.
And while I grin at this whimsical view,
I realize beneath, life's not so blue!

So let's dive deep, where the giggles abound,
With mermaids and dolphins, let's dance all around.
For beneath life's surface, joy can be found,
In the silly moments that life has astound!

Voices of Forgotten Paths

Tangled roots and silly shoes,
Whispering trees with playful views.
Where do we plan to roam and strut?
The map's a joke, we must be nuts!

Bouncing dreams in wobbly boats,
Chasing thoughts like wayward goats.
Every turn leads to a laugh,
Who knew the trail was a world of gaffs?

Silly signs and painted spots,
Dancing squirrels, and funny thoughts.
Each step tells a joke or two,
Laughter echoes, we're never blue!

Let's toast to paths we cannot find,
To the wanderers, a carefree mind!
In every giggle, a story's spun,
Life's a prank, and we've just begun!

The Landscape of Intent

In a field of mismatched socks,
Intentions grow like silly rocks.
A cartwheel here, a noodle dance,
Who knew life could be such a chance?

Plan the picnic, but bring a spoon,
For spaghetti sticks beneath the moon.
With ants as guests and clouds for shade,
We laugh and eat, no plans betrayed!

Goals float by like balloons on strings,
Watch them pop with foolish things.
Mistakes become the highlight reel,
In this crazy game, we all can feel!

So here's a toast to our grand design,
With chocolate cake and a side of wine.
Intentions funny, clear as day,
We'll wander boldly, come what may!

Starlit Adventures

Under twinkling lights, we roam,
With mismatched maps, we call it home.
Bouncing ideas like skipping stones,
In this night, our laughter's grown!

Starry skies holding our schemes,
Chasing dreams from silly themes.
With every stumble, we find delight,
In the moon's glow, we ignite the night!

Crazy wishes on shooting stars,
Silent giggles and oddly shaped cars.
Sideways glances, playful frowns,
Life's a stage, and we're the clowns!

Our starlit quest, a riotous spree,
Maps are for those who can't be free.
So here's our journey, unbound and true,
In this wild dance, we'll find our cue!

Labyrinths of Thought

In a maze of giggles and crazy schemes,
We stumble through our wacky dreams.
Round every corner, a joke awaits,
With every twist, our laughter celebrates!

Riddles twist like pretzel knots,
Thoughts diverge like tangled plots.
Finding the way seems quite absurd,
But oh, the tales that go unheard!

With compass wrong and laughter bright,
We wade through all the silly sights.
At every dead-end, we share a cheer,
For it's the journey that brings us here!

So let's embrace this joyful rut,
No straight paths meant for us nutty butts.
In the labyrinth of our funny quests,
We've found our laugh, and it truly rests!

Seeds of Belief

In a garden of dreams we play,
Where daisies whisper without delay.
A sunflower thinks it's a big, bold star,
While peanuts ponder just who they are.

We plant our hopes in shallow ground,
Expecting miracles to come around.
But all we grow are weeds so tall,
Who knew that faith could trip us all?

With each new sprout, we laugh and cheer,
Until the rabbit munches near.
Yet in this chaos, we truly find,
That life's a joke, and we're all blind!

So sprinkle love like seeds in air,
And giggle at the ups and despair.
For in this wild, absurd ballet,
It's laughter that lights our wiggly way.

Musings from the Edge of Existence

On the edge of dimensions, we sway,
With popcorn thoughts that roll away.
Gravity loses its iron grip,
As we float on ideas, a metaphorical trip.

What's the point of an endless day?
When socks disappear in a curious ballet.
We ponder life with half-eaten cake,
And through giggles, we'll suddenly wake.

We measure time with the ticks of a clock,
But our minds race like a comical flock.
Chasing shadows that wear silly hats,
While debating if we're just talking cats.

So let's stroll on this absurdity lane,
Collect curiosities like candy canes.
With humor as our guiding compass,
We'll discover the edge isn't so ominous.

The Language of Longing

In whispers, we speak of things unseen,
Like kittens arguing about who's mean.
Desires dance on the tip of our tongue,
As awkward verses are playfully sung.

A donut dreams of being a star,
While a coffee mug claims it's gone too far.
Lost in translations we giggle and sigh,
Longing for snacks as the minutes fly.

We scribble wishes on napkins and walls,
Where spaghetti falls in the grandest of stalls.
Our hearts yearn for joy and a silly romance,
In the language of longing, we throw our pants!

So let's toast to dreams that make us roar,
With every laugh, we open a door.
For in this wild lexicon, we find our beat,
That longing is just life's wobbly treat.

Pathways to the Unimagined

On roads of whimsy, we wander wide,
With rubber chickens at our side.
Each turn turns into a surprise,
As dancing squirrels plot their next rise.

We chase after moons made of cheese,
While tickled by a dandelion breeze.
The unexpected shines on every lane,
Where laughter's echoes wobble like rain.

Caution signs flash, "No Seriousness Here!"
As we juggle emotions with a splash of cheer.
The map to joy is scribbled in crayon,
With shortcuts through clouds and marzipan.

Let's skip through this uncharted terrain,
Finding wonders that are truly insane.
Because in this journey of giggles and glee,
We create a world where we're all just free.

The Odyssey of Self

In a ship made of rubber and dreams,
I sailed through the land of ice creams.
The map was just doodles, a child's delight,
Every wave whispered, 'You're doing it right!'

I met a wise turtle who played chess,
He said, 'It's a game! Don't take it a mess!'
With jellyfish knights and a dolphin queen,
We laughed 'til our bellies turned jellybean.

Every mirror was a funhouse twist,
Reflecting my dreams, none could be missed.
I danced with a crab who wore a top hat,
He clapped his claws—imagine that!

The odyssey taught me it's all a jest,
In finding myself, I found the best.
So here's to the laughs, the quirks, the play,
Self-discovery is the silliest way!

Embers of Passion

From ashes of boredom, a spark was born,
I tried cooking pasta—got burned, forlorn.
With flames dancing wildly, a fire so bright,
I yelled, 'Look, I'm cooking! Oh what a sight!'

A pot on my head, I called it a crown,
In my kingdom of chefs, I wouldn't back down.
I twirled in the kitchen like a wild chef-star,
Chaos erupted—my dance was bizarre!

The onion was crying, the garlic too shy,
I asked them, 'Join in!' but they said, 'Goodbye!'
With each chopping motion, the laughter took flight,
Dinner was laughter, a sight with delight.

In cooking this mess, I found my true scope,
The key was to laugh, to kindle some hope.
So here's to the embers in pots far and wide,
Ignite your own passion, wear it with pride!

Searching Through Time

I set my sights on a clock with a grin,
Tick-tock giggles, where shall we begin?
With a hop to the past, I tripped on a shoe,
Found dinosaurs dancing—that's something new!

A raptor in shades tried to teach me the moves,
With a jive and a shimmy, he certainly grooves.
I took a selfie with cavemen and glee,
Their bangs were way cooler—how could this be?

Then off to the future, in a flash I would zoom,
Met robots with humor—oh, how they could bloom!
They told me, 'Don't worry, just laugh at the flops,'
Time traveled better with giggles and hops.

In searching through time, I found a delight,
That laughter's the treasure, it shines ever bright.
So next time you ponder where you should roam,
Remember, the giggles always lead you home!

Finding the Unseen Light

In the closet, I searched for a ghost,
To share my snacks and maybe toast.
I found a sock with a smile so wide,
Turned out it's my buddy, my sock with pride!

We planned a party, the fridge was our stage,
With pickles and soda, a culinary rage.
The blender was singing a wild little tune,
We danced with the spoons, 'til we spoke to the moon!

I searched for the light that hid from my glance,
The flashlight was hiding, a little shy dance.
It beeped out a laugh, shining all around,
My unseen light was there, waiting to be found!

Together we glowed through the dark of the night,
Who knew that a sock could bring so much light?
So if you are lost in your quest for the beam,
Just check your own closet—it's wilder than dreams!

Spirals of Discovery

In a world where socks disappear,
I lost my sense of hey, oh dear!
Chasing wisdom like a squirrel,
Twirling thoughts in a dizzy whirl.

Maps are scribbled with crayon cheer,
X marks the spot, at least I hear!
I dug a hole for treasure rare,
Found a sandwich and some old hair.

Round and round in circles we go,
Seeking answers, don't you know?
A rubber chicken brings the fun,
Laughing out loud, we've just begun.

So let's embrace this tasty quest,
For giggles are the very best,
In spirals of nonsense, we'll confide,
Who needs logic, let's just ride!

The Map of the Heart

A treasure map drawn on my chest,
With arrows pointing to all the rest.
Hearts and stars, a doodle spree,
X's mark love, can't you see?

Commas pause through silly chatter,
Finding joy in what's the matter.
Each line a bumpy road to roam,
With every detour leading home.

Puns and riddles in every fold,
The secrets of joy can't be controlled.
A compass spinning wildly round,
In laughter's echo, true love is found.

So take this map, adventure near,
With giggles as our guiding sphere.
For in the maze of hearts we chart,
We find the fun, and that's the art!

The Alchemy of Dreams

Mixing potions with a wink,
In dreamland, we sip and think.
A pinch of giggle and a dash of cheer,
Sprinkle it all, and look who's here!

Turning pancakes into gold,
A magic secret never told.
Flying cats in a sky of cream,
Chasing bubbles, so it seems.

In this lab of goofy schemes,
Where nothing's real, but oh, it gleams!
Alchemy's done with flair and zest,
Transforming sleep into the best.

Join the circus of intertwining dreams,
Where nothing's quite as it seems.
With laughter as our only theme,
We'll dance along in the silvery beam!

Essence of the Journey

With mismatched shoes, I start to roam,
Finding joy makes the world feel like home.
A loopy path lined with silly sights,
Twinkling lights in the starry nights.

Curvy roads and twists galore,
Every turn reveals something more.
Jumping puddles, a leap of faith,
Splashing around, it's never too late.

Dancing through fields of daffodils,
Tickling the breeze with our silly thrills.
Every step, a chuckle bright,
In the essence of journey, we take flight.

So pack your giggles, let's depart,
For adventure thrives in the playful heart.
With laughter leading the way so free,
The essence of life is pure glee!

The Art of Discovery

In search of treasure, I seek and roam,
With maps and compasses that lead me home.
But lo! A wrong turn, I'm lost in a vine,
A salad of greens where pancakes should shine.

I find a butterfly, it starts to laugh,
Its wings a color palette, quite the gaffe!
Chasing after it, I trip on a root,
Stumbling forward, I land in a fruit.

Each twist and turn brings giggles anew,
Life's odd adventures, just think what we knew!
From pickles to pigeons, nothing's quite lame,
In the art of discovery, we play the game.

With jellybean maps and a giggle or two,
The world is my canvas, filled with bright hues.
So here's to the journey, the chuckles, the spree,
In the art of discovery, I just need a key!

Embracing Chaos

Today's schedule met chaos, oh what a sight,
Cats in the laundry, just daring to bite.
My socks disappear, like magic they flee,
Perhaps in the sock realm, they're wild and free.

I set out for coffee, but found a parade,
Dancing with llamas that never obeyed.
With confetti like rain, they twirled in delight,
I joined in the fest, what a wonderful night!

Juggling the chaos, I slip on a pie,
A splat on my face, oh me, oh my!
But laughter erupts, as I roll on the floor,
Embracing the chaos, who could ask for more?

In life's mix of madness, we twist and we shout,
With laughter we conquer, there's never a doubt.
So let's toast to the chaos, the flops and the thrills,
Embracing each moment, through mishaps and spills!

The Dance of Possibilities

In whimsical shoes, I twirl and I leap,
With dreams in my pocket, I dance and I peep.
Through puddles and rainbows, I spin with glee,
What if the grass is pink? Let it be!

Options abound like confetti in air,
Should I skate on bananas, or twirl like a bear?
With giggles and chuckles, I let freedom ring,
Every misstep becomes a wild new fling.

A chicken joins in, with moves of its own,
We shimmy and shake, in this dance, we've grown.
A disco ball shines on our funny parade,
In the dance of possibilities, we won't be afraid.

So take off your shoes, let's dance through the night,
With each twist and turn, let's savor the light.
For life is a stage with spots that shine bright,
In the dance of possibilities, everything's right!

The Horizon of Dreams

On a quest for my dreams, I set out one day,
With a suitcase of wishes and snacks on display.
But lo! A squirrel stole my sandwich with zest,
I'll chase that little rascal, it's part of my quest.

I climbed the tall mountain, or so I believed,
But tripped on my shoelace, how I deceived.
Rolling down gently, still grinning with glee,
Every tumble teaches, just wait, you will see.

At sunset, I ponder the glories ahead,
With bubbles and rainbows, I dance with the dread.
Each dream holds a story, a giggle, a scheme,
In the horizon of dreams, let's carry our beam.

So pack up those dreams, bring joy on the way,
With laughter and stories, we'll brighten the day.
For in the horizon where laughter is the theme,
Life's wild adventure is better, it seems!

The Silent Call of Horizons

In the distance, a horizon smiles,
Whispering secrets of countless miles.
I pack my bags, set out for fun,
Not sure if I'm lost or just on the run.

The sun winks down, a mischievous tease,
Chasing down ducks, or perhaps some bees.
I navigate with snacks and a map,
Hoping to find joy, not just a nap.

Around every corner, absurdities pop,
A dancing llama makes me stop!
"Is this the meaning?" I ponder aloud,
While wearing my breakfast, feeling so proud.

With laughter as fuel, I venture each day,
Chasing odd moments in a whimsical way.
Perhaps the quest is not wisely planned,
But isn't it grand? Just to understand!

Quest for Meaning

I armed myself with jellybeans,
In hopes of unraveling life's silly scenes.
With each bright color, a clue to find,
The meaning of life – or what's on my mind.

I stumbled on puzzles, all riddled and mixed,
Walking in circles, quite hopelessly fixed.
A bird squawked loudly, as if to say,
"Stop chasing your tail, let laughter lead the way!"

Finding wisdom in rubber duck races,
And snippets of joy in the silliest places.
So when in doubt, ditch the tomes,
And fill your head with giggles and gnomes!

In this absurd adventure, I finally decree,
The quest is the giggle, oh can't you see?
As I munch on my treats and count all my friends,
I realize that joy is where the fun never ends!

Journey to the Heart of Existence

I donned my hat and hiking boots,
Set off with dreams, laughter, and brutes.
The path of purpose paved by messes,
With squirrels as guides, their nutty successes.

Dancing past trees like they're in a ballet,
I wondered what thoughts would lead us astray.
A frog in a top hat croaked with glee,
"Life's a giggle, just come follow me!"

Onwards through confusion, I skip and slide,
With pie-in-the-face moments to giggle and glide.
Found wisdom in laughter, and joy in the absurd,
In every odd notion, I found my true word.

So here's to the journey, both wild and spry,
With hiccups and giggles, we'll never say die!
For the heart, it beats best when wrapped in delight,
Like a squirrel in a top hat, twinkling at night!

Unveiling Life's Mysteries

With a magnifying glass and a wobbly stance,
I dived into questions, hoping for chance.
What's under that rock? An old shoe? A cat?
Each mystery's thrilling, let's have a chat!

I found socks with questions, and then came the joke,
"Why did the chicken?" it started to poke.
In every odd moment resides a small thrill,
Beneath silly layers, life's lessons instill.

Caught in a riddle of everyday cheer,
With giggling clouds floating near,
Life's oddities beckon, and I gladly reply,
"Show me your secrets, I'm ready to fly!"

So here's to the laughter, the giggle, the noise,
In unveiling what matters, let's all find our joys.
With quips and odd moments, let's paint life absurd,
For in playful pursuits, our truth is stirred!

Paths of Destiny

In shoes too tight, I stroll with glee,
A map in hand, but lost I be.
A squirrel waves, a cat throws shade,
Are these the signs? My plans mislaid.

A signpost points, says 'This way fun!'
I flip a coin, the journey's begun.
With twists and turns, I laugh and trip,
If purpose's here, I need a sip!

Detours squeeze my dreams like figs,
I dance with cacti and juggle jigs.
Edible flowers bloom with grace,
Are they my goal? A veggie race?

But with each step, I find a cheer,
Life's a game, I couldn't steer.
If destiny's a puzzle vast,
I'll eat the pieces, have a blast!

Whispers of Ambition

In a coffee shop, I sip and sigh,
My dreams take flight, then crash and die.
The barista winks, my latte's hot,
Is she my muse, or just a plot?

Goals on paper, wish upon stars,
I aim for Mars, but end up in bars.
With laughter loud and friends close by,
Who knew success would taste like pie?

I tried my best to look so smart,
But tripped on wisdom—don't ask me how.
Ambition's whispers turn to guffaws,
Life's a circus, I applaud the flaws!

Yet still I chase that elusive dream,
With rubber chickens, I sell ice cream.
So here's to missteps, happy falls,
For in the laughter, purpose calls!

Echoes of the Soul's Call

My heart speaks softly, then yells aloud,
Dressed as a chicken, I strut so proud.
With feathers bright, I dance in place,
Who knew deep thoughts could join the race?

Echoes of wisdom, a giggly tune,
I search for truth under a bright moon.
The stars are snickering, so bold and bright,
Maybe my purpose's within their light?

I ponder aloud while I pick my nose,
Is enlightenment hiding with garden gnomes?
So here's to the voices that make me smile,
Let's celebrate weirdness, let's go that mile!

In moments strange, I grab a slice,
If the soul's a dance, I'll roll the dice.
With laughter ringing through starlit halls,
I'll chase my echoes, answering calls!

Seeking the Golden Horizon

Chasing sunsets on a broken bike,
Stumbling forward, but hey, it's a hike!
The golden hue, where dreams unfold,
Is that my fortune or just fools' gold?

With a map from 1981,
I guess I'm lost—hardly a fun run.
Each hill I climb feels like a joke,
Is purpose near? Or did I choke?

I barter snacks with clouds up high,
The horizon laughs as it rolls on by.
A seagull swoops, steals my last chip,
If you can't beat 'em, join the trip!

In search of gold that sparkles and shines,
I find a treasure in cheesy lines.
So here's to laughs and the paths we find,
For humor's the gold that ties us, entwined!

Hearts in Motion

Bouncing here and bouncing there,
A heart that just won't sit in a chair.
It trips on dreams, spills on the floor,
Chasing giggles, always wanting more.

With every hop, it tells a joke,
A rubber chicken wrapped in a cloak.
It dances wildly, makes us grin,
In the chaos of joy, we all win.

Caught in a swirl of color and cheer,
It sings of the silly, loud and clear.
Each beat is a melody, quirky and bright,
Twirling through life like it's pure delight.

So let your heart waltz, don't hold it tight,
Give it some wiggle, bask in the light.
In the circus of living, with laughs all around,
Hearts in motion, where joy can be found.

The Light Beyond Shadows

There's a hallway of funny, with bright polka dots,
Where shadows are sneaky, and tie funny knots.
The lights flicker, giggling like silly old fools,
And shadows wear socks, which are just not for mules.

A beam so bright comes skipping along,
It twirls with the shadows; oh, can't be wrong!
It chuckles at darkness, takes it to play,
Forming shadows that dance in a whimsical way.

In this vibrant circus, we all join the fun,
Chasing the shadows 'til the day is done.
They hide behind laughter, peeking to see,
The light that reveals what we wish to be.

So shine your glow with pure, endless zest,
For the shadows are funny; they too need a rest.
Together we laugh in the blare of delight,
In the glow of good humor, all wrongs feel so right.

Threads of Hope

We weave with laughter, colorful threads,
Stitching up dreams in the silliest spreads.
A needle that dances, skipping a beat,
Turning dull fabric into something neat.

With hope on a spool, we tug and we tease,
Crafting a tale that floats in the breeze.
It's a quilt of joy, patched from the past,
Where each wacky stitch has a tale to cast.

In the fabric of moments, we find our way,
Sewing our stories, come what may.
So unravel the drab and embrace the bright,
For each thread of laughter brings pure delight.

Here's to the fabric that holds us so tight,
Threads of hope giggling, sparkling with light.
In the loom of together, we'll find our blend,
Sewn up with joy, it's a pattern to send.

Whispering Intentions

In the corners of chatter, intentions whisper loud,
With a tickle of mischief buried in the crowd.
They giggle in secret, flirting with fate,
Transforming the mundane into something great.

Each intention dances with a flick of the wrist,
Wearing a tutu, kissed by a mist.
They float like balloons, tangled in a breeze,
Whispering jokes that bring us to knees.

Oh, watch as they twirl, like fireflies at night,
Filling the air with a chuckle, so light.
In the symphony of wishes, they play a role,
Funny little whispers that fill up the soul.

So let's share intentions wrapped up in fun,
For life's just a party, and we've only begun.
With laughter as fuel, we'll dance uninterrupted,
In a world of whispers, our dreams are erupted.

Quest for Meaning

I woke up one day with a question in mind,
What's the point of my life? I couldn't find.
So I searched in the fridge for answers and cheese,
But all I found was a sandwich and a sneeze.

I tried asking my cat, she just stared at me,
She's got nine lives, what could she decree?
With a wiggle and a purr, she turned away,
Guess she's busy searching for her own buffet.

I set out to find what makes me feel whole,
Perhaps it's a donut or maybe a role.
Dancing in circles, I slip on the floor,
Turns out, the purpose is to explore more.

So here I am, with my mind in a spin,
Life's a pie chart, and I want my win.
With laughter and joy in each silly quest,
I conclude that the journey is truly the best.

Echoes of Destiny

They say fate whispers softly in the night,
But I think it giggles, then takes flight.
I follow the sound down a winding old road,
Hoping to find what lightens the load.

A sign says 'Destiny,' I stop for a peek,
It's just a raccoon with a cheesy critique.
He's got a flair for dramatic well-played,
And I wonder if destiny's just well-laid.

I bump into folks, each with a wild scheme,
A yo-yo magician or a banana dream.
We laugh and we ponder, who's got the say?
Is it fate or just luck- that guides our way?

As echoes of laughter ring out in the air,
It dawns on me that it's fun we all share.
For lost in the chaos, a truth shines so bright,
The journey with friends is the purest delight.

Threads of Tomorrow

I've woven my dreams into colors so bold,
A patchwork of laughs and some stories retold.
Each thread has a giggle, a blush, and a sigh,
But some of them fray, what a comical lie!

I dropped a few stitches while searching for glue,
Turns out, my ambition was only for stew.
With flour on my hands and a wink in my eye,
I baked my great plans and hoped they'd fly high.

The universe chuckled, said, 'Try something new,'
So I knitted some socks, but they turned out askew.
A sock for a hand and a glove for my foot,
I think I've discovered my own fashion truth!

Now the threads of tomorrow are tangled and neat,
Each twist is a memory, each knot is a treat.
With laughter as yarn and love as the seam,
I'll stitch up adventure, life's glorious dream.

Chasing Shadows of Purpose

I set out one night with a lantern in hand,
To chase down my purpose, oh wasn't it grand?
But all that I caught was a shadow, not me,
Just a rogue little bug dancing low by a tree.

I tripped over laughter and bumped into fate,
It said with a grin, 'Your journey's first date.'
We had cupcakes and giggles under the stars,
By morning, I found I was stuck with my car.

With mirrors and wishes, reflections in streams,
I pondered my life and my wild pie dreams.
In shadows, I stumbled, then danced and I spun,
Turns out, the fun part was all of the fun.

So here's my advice if you ever feel lost,
Chase shadows of purpose, but don't count the cost.
For laughter and joy are worth every glance,
In the dance of the moment, join in the prance.

Stardust and Aspirations

In a galaxy of dreams, we zoom,
Chasing hopes like meteors that loom.
With wands of laughter, we reach for stars,
Mapping out chaos in our little cars.

We twirl with giggles in cosmic glee,
In search of treasures, oh where could they be?
With silly hats and our starry plans,
We'll dance in space with furry cans.

An alien chef serves up moon pie,
While a comet asks, 'Why do we even try?'
We shrug and munch on starlit bread,
Dreaming of adventures ahead!

Each twinkle's a wink from fate it seems,
As we launch our strange and funny schemes.
So here's to laughter in the cosmic swirl,
As we navigate life's whirling twirl!

Navigating the Nebula of Being

In the nebula we float and soar,
Pondering purpose, oh what a chore!
With giggles and bubbles we traverse the void,
Accidental astronauts, humor deployed.

We dodge asteroids and quirky grins,
Sailing through rifts where confusion begins.
An echo of laughter rings in the air,
As we search for meaning in a cosmic fair.

The stars wink at us with sly little charms,
While we juggle thoughts and imaginary arms.
Why'd the nebula become such a maze?
Just ask the dust bunnies that brighten our days!

So let's twirl through the chaos, have some fun,
With interstellar secrets we can't outrun.
In this wild array of colors and dreams,
We'll dance through the cosmos, or so it seems!

Footprints in Time

We dance through the sands where moments reside,
Leaving footprints of laughter with each joyful stride.
Time splashes back like a playful wave,
Tickling our toes, how we misbehave!

Each footprint tells tales of giggles and fun,
Of mischief and magic 'neath the bright sun.
The clocks just chuckle as we race by,
They can't keep up, oh me, oh my!

Sketching our journey, a pattern bizarre,
In a world where wisdom is just a big spar.
Tick-tock, tick-tock, the sound of our quest,
As we look for the jokes, it's the very best!

So we run in circles, round and around,
With our silly antics, blissfully unbound.
The footprints we leave are funky and bright,
A comical map of our wild delight!

Unraveling the Tapestry of Life

In a world woven with colors so bright,
We tug at the threads, what a hilarious sight!
With a wink and a grin, we start to unwind,
Finding joy in the knots that we leave behind.

Each layer unravels a mystery grand,
With patterns of laughter made by our hand.
We trip on the yarn, oh what a surprise,
As the tapestry giggles and dances with sighs.

From pom-poms to tassels, the fabric's alive,
As we stitch our own stories, a quirky hive.
Why chase the meaning when laughter's the key?
It's a patchwork of silly, come dance along with me!

So let's weave a dance of inspired delight,
In the tapestry of life, where humor shines bright.
No patterns too strange, no threads too thin,
Unraveling joy, oh let the fun begin!

The Fire Within

I woke up today with a spark in my eye,
Determined to soar, not just to fly.
But coffee was missing, oh what a plight,
I pondered my purpose, fueled by caffeine light.

With toast in my hand, I started to dream,
Could my life be more than just breakfast themes?
A whisper of passion, a giggle, a snort,
Let's dance through the chaos, in hilarious court.

I chased after llamas, they laughed as they ran,
Deciding that maybe I'm part of the plan.
In socks and sandals, I whipped out my phone,
And snapped all my missteps, my laughter was grown.

So here's to the fire that's fueled by delight,
We'll search for our purpose, in day and in night.
With humor as compass, we'll find our own way,
And toast with our laughter—what a splendid buffet!

A Symphony of Intentions

The orchestra played, but they were off-key,
A symphony crafted for only me.
With kazoo in hand, I joined in the fun,
Making music from chaos, my day's just begun.

I tripped on the stage, but who needs a plan?
A tickle of laughter, oh, what a grand jam!
With drumsticks for chopsticks, I dined in delight,
Dinner table's a concert—treats take flight!

The conductor threw notes like confetti in air,
I joined the parade, with a wink and a flare.
In a world full of rhythms, let's dance to our song,
Embrace every mishap, it's where we belong.

So here's to our tunes, both silly and grand,
With intentions like melodies, let's take a stand.
In this symphonic journey, laughter does lead,
Together we'll flourish, yes indeed, yes indeed!

Beneath the Stars of Wonder

Under a moon that giggled with glee,
I pondered my fate, as a star leaned on me.
"Why not bounce on the clouds?" it said with a twinkle,
"Life's more than a puzzle—it's a whimsical sprinkle!"

I packed up my troubles, tossed them in space,
And floated on wishes, with a sheepish embrace.
There's truth in the laughter, silly and bright,
For under these stars, we'll dance through the night.

The comets all chuckled as I twirled and spun,
With wishful intentions, joining in the fun.
The cosmos conspired, a galactic cheer,
"Just be your own quirk—your purpose is near!"

So let's twinkle like stardust, both vivid and bold,
Find joy in the laughter that brightens our fold.
Beneath all the wonders, with spirits entwined,
We'll celebrate "us"—let our true selves unwind!

A Tapestry of Aspirations

I stitched up my dreams with threads of pure cheer,
A tapestry woven, with joy as the seer.
"Who needs a degree?" I mused with delight,
As I crafted my journey, with giggles in sight.

With needle and thread, I fashioned my goal,
A quilt made of laughter, that's how I roll.
With patches of whimsy and loops of bright hues,
I wrapped up my hopes in polka-dot blues.

The fabric of life is a comical blend,
Of mishaps and triumphs—on laughter, depend!
With every new stitch, I embraced every laugh,
As our aspirations form a silly warm bath.

So here's to our tapestry, colorful, bold,
A patchwork of stories and smiles to unfold.
In crafting our passions, let chuckles unwind,
For woven together, fulfillment we'll find!

Beneath the Canopy of Possibility

Beneath the leaves of chance we prance,
With squirrels debating the best dance.
They twirl and spin, round and round,
Lost in dreams, with snacks they're bound.

A bird sings loud with a cheeky glare,
While ants plot tea parties without a care.
They invite the worms, for laughs and snacks,
As sunlight spills in all its relaxing tracks.

We chase the breeze, like a game of tag,
And laugh at clouds that look like a drag.
With silly hats and goofy styles,
We craft new plans with silly smiles.

So come along, you curious soul,
Join this chaotic and whimsical stroll.
In the woods of wonder, we'll find our way,
Where fun is king, and serious? Nay!

The Alchemy of Becoming

In a lab of dreams, we mix a stew,
Of giggles, wiggles, and a bit of glue.
We'll zoom through time on a paper plane,
And chase the rainbows with playful disdain.

With goggles on, we turn things bright,
Like socks that dance on a Tuesday night.
We'll brew a potion of laughter and cheer,
Stirred with mischief, oh dear, oh dear!

Each fail is gold, we're alchemists bold,
Turning spills into stories that should be told.
With bubble wands and candy canes,
We'll craft our futures sans any chains.

So mix your whims, let the fun overflow,
With every blunder, we'll steal the show.
In this lab of life, let's be quite a pair,
Creating magic in the wacky air!

Portraits of Potential

We paint with colors that twirl and glide,
With cheeky brushes, we've nothing to hide.
Each splash is a giggle, a hint of delight,
As we doodle our dreams under the moonlight.

The canvas wobbles, but we hold it tight,
With scribbles and squiggles, a comical sight.
Our highs are like kites, our lows a fun trip,
As we bounce through life, joyful in our grip.

Each stroke tells a tale, both silly and true,
Of penguins in suits and a dancing shoe.
With laughter as paint, we craft what we see,
In this quirky gallery we call 'You and Me'.

So hang your portraits on the walls of your heart,
Embrace your potential, it's just the start.
For a masterpiece lives in the giggles we share,
In a world colorful, fun, and full of flair!

The Rhythm of the Quest

March to the beat of a kazoo parade,
With rhythms and rhymes that never will fade.
We strut and we dance, on a quest so grand,
With flip-flops squeaking, oh isn't it grand?

The treasure we seek? Candy-coated bliss,
With chocolate rivers, oh what a hit miss.
We'll share all our stories with sparkles and flair,
As we wander the valleys, without a care.

With maps made of pizza, we'll chart our way,
Through giggles and snorts, oh what a play!
In every step, a rhythm unfolds,
The melody's wacky, but the heart never scolds.

So join in the fun, let's skip and sway,
In this rhythm of life, let's dance and play.
For as we quest, we find the best jest,
A carnival ride in this whimsical fest!

www.ingramcontent.com/pod-product-compliance
Lightning Source LLC
Chambersburg PA
CBHW070751220426
43209CB00083B/882